THE GODHEAD

Elwin Shull, EdS

World rights reserved. This book or any portion thereof may not be copied or reproduced in any form or manner whatever, except as provided by law, without the written permission of the publisher, except by a reviewer who may quote brief passages in a review.

The author assumes full responsibility for the accuracy of all facts and quotations as cited in this book. The opinions expressed in this book are the author's personal views and interpretations, and do not necessarily reflect those of the publisher.

This book is provided with the understanding that the publisher is not engaged in giving spiritual, legal, medical, or other professional advice. If authoritative advice is needed, the reader should seek the counsel of a competent professional.

Copyright © 2021 Elwin Shull, EdS
Copyright © 2021 TEACH Services, Inc.
ISBN-13: 978-1-4796-1298-7 (Paperback)
ISBN-13: 978-1-4796-1299-4 (ePub)
Library of Congress Control Number: 2021904246

All Bible text references are taken from the King James Version of the Bible unless otherwise stated. Public domain.

Bible text references labeled (NKJV) are taken from the New King James Version® of the Bible. Copyright © 1982 by Thomas Nelson. Used by permission. All rights reserved.

Published by

www.TEACHServices.com • (800) 367-1844

DEDICATION

Dedicated to the Father, Son, and Holy Spirit who in love created thinking and rational beings.

TABLE OF CONTENTS

The Word "Godhead" in Scripture 9

What Scripture Tells Us
   of The Godhead 10

If God Is One God, Why and Where
   Does He Speak of Himself
   as Plural? 13

How Can Three Be One? 17

Does The Bible Say That Jesus Is God? . . 18

Does the Bible Say That the Holy
   Spirit Is God? 20

What Are Some of the Attributes that
   the Godhead Have in Common? 22

Members of the Godhead Have
   Person Characteristics 39

The Godhead Is Love 48

Jesus Gave His Life as an Example
   of the Love of the Godhead. 53

God's Moral Law Can Also Be
   Summarized by One Greek
   Word—Agape (Godlike Love) 55

The Godhead Does Not Change 59

Biblical Definition of Sin. 61

Where Sin Originated 63

Love Turned Inward Results in Sin 66

Some of the Godhead's Words that
   Help Us Overcome the Sin
   of Love Turned Inward 69

The Godhead Pleads for Our
   Repentance. 72

The Godhead Promises Good and
   Well-Being to All Who Keep
   Their Commandments. 75

The Godhead Desires All to be Saved . . . 78

The Godhead's Warnings to All
   Who Sin, and Keep Not Their
   Commandments 80

The Godhead's Strange Act
   On Unrepentant Self-Lovers 82

Biblical Explanation of the
   Second Death 84

Writers Inspired by the Godhead
    Give Examples of People that
    Delight Them 87

Appendix 1 . . . . *91*

Appendix 2 . . . . *97*

About the Author *104*

THE WORD "GODHEAD" IN SCRIPTURE

"Forasmuch then as we are offspring of God, we ought not to think that the Godhead is like unto gold, or silver, or stone graven by art and man's device" (Acts 17:29).

"For the invisible things of him from the creation of the world are clearly seen, being understood by the things that are made, *even* his eternal power and Godhead; so that they are without excuse" (Rom. 1:20).

"For in him [Christ] dwelleth all the fullness of the Godhead bodily" (Col. 2:9).

WHAT SCRIPTURE TELLS US OF THE <u>GODHEAD</u>

"*Touching* the Almighty, we cannot find him out" (Job 37:23).

"Canst thou by searching find out God? Canst thou find out the Almighty unto perfection? It *is* as high as heaven; what canst thou do? Deeper than hell; what canst thou know? The measure thereof is longer than the earth, and broader than the sea" (Job 11:7–9).

"O the depth of the riches both of the wisdom and knowledge of God! how unsearchable *are* his judgments, and his ways past finding out! For who has known the mind of the Lord? or who has become his counselor?" (Rom. 11:33–34).

"My thoughts *are* not your thoughts, neither are your ways my ways, saith the LORD, For *as* the heavens are higher than the earth, so are my ways higher than your ways, and my thoughts than your thoughts" (Isa. 55:8–9).

"*There is* no searching of his understanding" (Isa. 40:28).

"No man can find out the work that God maketh from the beginning to the end" (Eccles. 3:11).

"Then I beheld all the work of God, that a man cannot find out the work that is done under the sun: …though a wise *man* think to know it, yet shall he not be able to find *it*" (Eccles. 8:17).

"Without controversy great is the mystery of godliness" (1 Tim. 3:16).

"The secret *things* belong to the LORD our God: but those *things which* are revealed *belong* to us" (Deut. 29:29).

God is beyond human comprehension. God is infinite. If we understood all about God, He would cease to be God in our sight. God is infinitely higher than us. Therefore, we should not expect to be able to fully understand Him. We cannot comprehend infinity, eternity, or for that matter gravity, light, electricity, quarks, natural physical laws, Biblical moral laws, or living things coming into existence, but evidence of a loving designer God and His reality is all around us.

IF GOD IS ONE GOD, WHY AND WHERE DOES HE SPEAK OF HIMSELF AS PLURAL?

"God said, Let us make man in our image" (Gen. 1:26).

"And the LORD God said, Behold, the man is become as one of us" (Gen. 3:22).

"Let us go down, and confound their language" (Gen. 11:7).

"Also I heard the voice of the Lord, saying, Whom shall I send, and who will go for us?" (Isa. 6:8).

In Hebrew the word for God in Genesis 1:26 is *Elohim*. It is a plural noun that is used more than 2,700 times in the Old Testament. This means that the Holy Spirit inspired authors to use the plural *Elohim* about 10 times more often that the singular, *El*, when they describe God.

SCRIPTURE MENTIONS THE FATHER, THE SON, AND THE HOLY SPIRIT TOGETHER AS INDIVIDUALS IN MORE THAN 60 PASSAGES. SOME ARE GIVEN AS FOLLOWS:

"I [the Son] have not spoken in secret from the beginning; from the time that it was, there *am* I; and now the Lord [the Father], and his Spirit [Holy Spirit] hath sent me [the Son]" (Isa. 48:16).

"Go ye therefore, and teach all nations, baptizing them in the name of the Father, and of the Son, and of the Holy Ghost" (Matt. 28:19).

"The Holy Ghost descended in a bodily shape like a dove upon Him [Jesus], and a voice [Father] came from heaven which said, Thou art my beloved Son in whom I am well pleased" (Luke 3:22).

"God giveth not the Spirit by measure *unto him*. The Father loveth the Son" (John 3:34–35).

"The Comforter, *which is* the Holy Ghost whom the Father will send in my [Jesus] name, he shall teach" (John 14:26).

"The God of our fathers raised up Jesus, whom ye slew and hanged on a tree… And we are witnesses of these things; and *so is* also the Holy Ghost, whom God hath given to them that obey him" (Acts 5:30, 32–33).

"Now I beseech you, brethren, for the Lord Jesus Christ's sake, and for the love of the Spirit, that ye strive together with your prayers to God for me" (Rom. 15:30).

"The grace of the Lord Jesus Christ, and the love of God, and the communion of the Holy Ghost, *be* with you all" (2 Cor. 13:14).

"For through him [Jesus], we both have access by one Spirit unto the Father" (Eph. 2:18).

"Grieve not the Holy Spirit of God…even as God for Christ's sake hath forgiven you" (Eph. 4:30, 32).

"The blood of Christ, who through the eternal Spirit offered himself without spot to God" (Heb. 9:14).

"God the Father, through sanctification of the Spirit, unto obedience and sprinkling of the blood of Jesus" (1 Pet 1:2).

"Praying in the Holy Ghost, keep yourselves in the love of God, looking for the mercy of our Lord Jesus" (Jude 20–21).

HERE ARE SEVERAL OTHER TEXTS YOU CAN LOOK UP ON THIS SUBJECT:

Matthew 3:16–17; John 14:16–17; Acts 2:32–33; Romans 14:17–18; Romans 15:13–17; 1 Corinthians 2:8–10; 1 Corinthians 6:10–11; 1 Corinthians 12:4–6; 2 Corinthians 1:21–22; 2 Corinthians 3:3–6; Gal 2:21–3:2; Galatians 4:4–7; Ephesians 3:14–16; Ephesians 5:18–20; Colossians 1:6–8; 1 Thessalonians 1:1–6; 1 Thessalonians 5:18–19; Hebrews 6:4–6; 1 John 3:23–24; 1 John 4:13–14.

HOW CAN THREE BE ONE?

"There is neither male nor female: for ye are all one in Christ Jesus" (Gal. 3:28).

"That they all [Christ's followers] may be one; as thou Father, *art* in me, and I in thee, that they also may be one in us" (John 17:21).

"Therefore shall a man leave his father and his mother, and shall cleave unto his wife: and they shall be one" (Gen. 2:24).

"I and *my* Father are one" (John 10:30).

"Holy Father, keep through thine own name those whom thou hast given me, that they may be one, as we are [one]" (John 17:11).

DOES THE BIBLE SAY THAT JESUS IS GOD?

"And God said to Moses, I AM THAT I AM" (Exod. 3:14).

"Jesus said unto them, Verily, verily, I say unto you, Before Abraham was, I am" (John 8:58).

"In the beginning was the Word, and the Word was with God, and the Word was God...And the Word was made flesh, and dwelt among us, (and we beheld his glory, the glory as the only begotten" (John 1:1, 14).

"But unto the Son *he* [God] *saith*, Thy throne, O God, *is* for ever and ever" (Heb. 1:8).

"For in him [Christ] dwelleth all the fulness of the Godhead bodily" (Col. 2:9).

"They shall call his name Emmanuel, which being interpreted is God with us" (Matt. 1:23).

"For unto us a child is born, unto us a Son is given…and His name shall be called Wonderful, Counsellor, The mighty God, The everlasting Father, The Prince of Peace" (Isa. 9:6).

"Looking for that blessed hope, and the glorious appearing, of the great God and our Savior Jesus Christ" (Titus 2:13).

"Christ Jesus: Who, being in the form of God, thought it not robbery to be equal with God" (Phil. 2:5–6).

"That at the name of Jesus every knee should bow, of things in heaven, and *things* in earth, and *things* under the earth; And that every tongue should confess that Jesus Christ *is* Lord, to the glory of God the Father" (Phil. 2:10–11).

"Hereby perceive we the love *of God*, because he laid down his life for us" (1 John 3:16).

"The Lamb [Jesus] shall overcome them: for he is Lord of lords, and King of kings" (Rev. 17:14).

DOES THE BIBLE SAY THAT THE HOLY SPIRIT IS GOD?

"Why hath Satan filled thine heart to lie to the Holy Ghost...thou hast not lied unto men, but unto God" (Acts 5:3–4).

"Know ye not that ye are the temple of God, and *that* the Spirit of God dwelleth in you?" (1 Cor. 3:16).

"What? Know ye not that your body is the temple of the Holy Ghost *which is* in you" (1 Cor. 6:19).

"For ye are the temple of the living God; as God hath said, I will dwell in them, and walk in *them*; and I will be their God, and they shall be my people" (2 Cor. 6:16).

"Surely the Lord GOD will do nothing, but he revealeth his secret unto his servants the prophets" (Amos 3:7).

"For prophecy came not in old time by the will of man: but holy men of God spake *as they were* moved by the Holy Ghost" (2 Pet. 1:21).

"All scripture *is* given by inspiration of God" (2 Tim. 3:16).

"All manner of sin and blasphemy shall be forgiven unto men: but the blasphemy *against* the Holy Ghost shall not be forgiven unto men. And whosoever speaketh a word against the Son of man, it shall be forgiven him: but whosoever speaketh against the Holy Ghost, it shall not be forgiven him" (Matt. 12:31–32).

"All sins shall be forgiven unto the sons of men, and blasphemies wherewith soever they shall blaspheme: But he that shall blaspheme against the Holy Ghost hath never forgiveness" (Mark 3:28–29).

"And whosoever shall speak a word against the Son of man, it shall be forgiven him: but unto him that blasphemeth against the Holy Ghost it shall not be forgiven" (Luke 12:10).

WHAT ARE SOME OF THE ATTRIBUTES THAT THE GODHEAD HAVE IN COMMON?

THEY ARE OMNIPOTENT:

FATHER: "Ah Lord GOD! behold, thou hast made the heaven and the earth by thy great power and stretched out arm, *and* there is nothing too hard for thee... Behold, I *am* the Lord, the God of all flesh: is there any thing too hard for me?" (Jer. 32:17, 27).

"With men this is impossible; but with God all things are possible" (Matt. 19:26).

JESUS: "And Jesus came and spake unto them, saying, All power is given unto me in heaven and in earth" (Matt. 28:18).

"Who is the image of the invisible God... For by him were all things created, that are in heaven, and that are in earth, visible and invisible...all things were created by him, and for him: And he is before all things, and by him all things consist" (Col. 1:15–17).

HOLY SPIRIT: "By his spirit he hath garnished the heavens" (Job 26:13).

"And there shall come forth a rod out of the stem of Jesse, and a Branch shall grow out of his roots: And the spirit of the LORD shall rest upon him, the spirit of wisdom and understanding, the spirit of counsel and might, the spirit of knowledge and of the fear of the LORD" (Isa. 11:1–2).

"And the angel answered and said unto her, The Holy Ghost shall come upon thee, and the power of the Highest shall overshadow thee" (Luke 1:35).

"Wherefore I give you to understand, that no man speaking by the Spirit of God calleth Jesus accursed: and that no man can say Jesus is Lord, but by the Holy Ghost" (1 Cor. 12:3).

THEY ARE OMNISCIENT:

FATHER: "His understanding *is* infinite" (Ps. 147:5).

"*I am* God…Declaring the end from the beginning, and from ancient times *the things* that are not *yet* done" (Isa. 46:9–10).

"God is greater than our heart, and knoweth all things" (1 John 3:20).

JESUS: "Of the mystery of God, and of the Father, and of Christ; In whom are hid all the treasures of wisdom and knowledge" (Col. 2:2–3).

HOLY SPIRIT: "…God hath revealed *them* unto us by his Spirit: for the Spirit searcheth all things, yea, the deep things of God… even so the things of God knoweth no man, but the Spirit of God" (1 Cor. 2:10–11).

"Who hath directed the Spirit of the LORD, or *being* his counsellor hath taught him? With whom took he counsel, and *who* instructed him, and taught him in the path of judgment, and taught him knowledge, and shewed to him the way of understanding?" (Isa. 40:13–14).

"When he, the Spirit of truth, is come…he will shew you things to come" (John 16:13).

THEY ARE OMNIPRESENT:

FATHER: "Whither shall I go from thy spirit? or whither shall I flee from thy presence? If I ascend up into heaven, thou *art* there, if I make my bed in hell, behold thou *art there. If* I take the winds of the morning, *and* dwell in the uttermost parts of the sea; Even there shall thy hand lead me, and thy right hand shall hold me" (Ps. 139:7–12).

"The eyes of the LORD *are* in every place, beholding the evil and the good" (Prov. 15:3).

JESUS: "For where two or three are gathered together in my name, there am I in the midst of them" (Matt. 18:20).

"Lo, I am with you always, *even* unto the end of the world" (Matt. 28:20).

HOLY SPIRIT: "Whither shall I go from thy Spirit? or whither shall I flee from thy presence?…For thou hast possessed my reins: thou hast covered me in my mother's womb" (Ps. 139:7, 13).

"*Even* the Spirit of truth…ye know him; for he dwelleth with you, and shall be in you" (John 14:17).

THEY ARE ETERNAL:

FATHER: "For thus saith the high and lofty One that inhabiteth eternity, whose name *is* Holy" (Isa. 57:15).

"Before the mountains were brought forth, or ever thou hadst formed the earth and the world, even from everlasting to everlasting, thou *art* God" (Ps. 90:2).

"*Abraham*...called there on the name of the LORD, the everlasting God" (Gen. 21:33).

"The eternal God *is thy* refuge, and underneath *are* the everlasting arms" (Deut. 33:27).

JESUS: "In the beginning was the Word, and the Word was with God, and the Word was God" (John 1:1).

"But thou Bethleham Ephratah...out of thee shall he come forth unto me *that is* to be ruler in Israel; whose going forth *have been* from old, from everlasting" (Micah 5:2).

"...I am the first and the last; I *am* he that liveth, and was dead, and behold, I am alive for evermore" (Rev. 1:17–18).

HOLY SPIRIT: "How much more shall the blood of Christ, who through the eternal Spirit offered himself without spot to God" (Heb. 9:14).

THEY ARE HOLY:

FATHER: "But the Lord of hosts shall be exalted in judgment, and God that is holy" (Isa. 5:16).

"And now I [Jesus] am no more in the world but these are in the world, and I come to thee. Holy Father, keep through thine own name" (John 17:11).

"Exalt the LORD our God, and worship at his holy hill, for the Lord our God *is* holy" (Ps. 99:9).

JESUS: "But ye denied the Holy One and the Just, and desired a murderer to be granted unto you" (Acts 3:14).

"For of a truth against thy holy child Jesus, whom thou hast anointed…and that signs and wonders may be done by the name of thy holy child Jesus" (Acts 4:27, 30).

HOLY SPIRIT: "And grieve not the holy Spirit of God, whereby ye are sealed" (Eph. 4:30). (Many times throughout the Bible the Spirit is called the Holy Spirit or Holy Ghost.)

THEY ARE POWER:

FATHER: "…For there is no power but of God" (Rom. 13:1).

"It is not for you to know the times of the seasons, which the Father hath put in his own power" (Acts 1:7).

"To the only wise God our Savior, be glory and majesty, dominion and power" (Jude 25).

JESUS: "How God anointed Jesus of Nazareth with the Holy Ghost and with power" (Acts 10:38).

Jesus came and spake unto them saying, All power is given unto me in heaven and in earth" (Matt. 28:18).

"I lay down my life…I have power to lay it down, and I have power to take it again." (John 10:17–18).

HOLY SPIRIT: "Truly I am full of power by the spirit of the Lord" (Mic. 3:8).

"Ye shall receive power, after that the Holy Ghost is come upon you" (Acts 1:8).

"Through mighty signs and wonders, by the power of the Spirit of God" (Rom. 15:19).

THEY CREATE:

FATHER: "Hast thou not known? Hast thou not heard *that* the everlasting God, the Lord, the Creator of the ends of the earth" (Isa. 40:28).

JESUS: "Hath in these last days spoken unto us by *his* Son…by whom also he made the worlds" (Heb. 1:2).

"All things were made by him; and without him was not anything made that was made" (John 1:3).

HOLY SPIRIT: "And the Spirit of God moved upon the face of the waters" (Gen. 1:2).

"By his Spirit he garnished the heavens" (Job 26:13).

"The Spirit of God hath made me, and the breath of the Almighty hath given me life" (Job 33:4).

"Thou sendest forth thy spirit, they are created" (Ps. 104:30).

THEY ARE LIFE:

FATHER: "The breath of the Almighty hath given me life" (Job 33:4).

"For as the Father hath life in himself; so hath he given to the Son to have life in himself" (John 5:26).

JESUS: "In him [Jesus] was life; and the life was the light of men" (John 1:4).

"Jesus saith unto him, I am the way, the truth, and the life" (John 14:6).

"God hath given to us eternal life, and this life is in his Son" (1 John 5:11).

HOLY SPIRIT: "But the Spirit *is* life" (Rom. 8:10).

"But he that soweth to the Spirit shall of the Spirit reap life everlasting" (Gal. 6:8).

THEY RESURRECT:

FATHER: "And killed the Prince of life, whom God hath raised from the dead" (Acts 3:15).

"Paul, an apostle, (not of men, neither by man, but by Jesus Christ, and God the

Father, who raised him from the dead)" (Gal. 1:1).

JESUS: "I am the resurrection, and the life: he that believeth in me, though he were dead, yet shall he live" (John 11:25).

"For as in Adam all die, even so in Christ shall be made alive" (1 Cor. 15:22).

HOLY SPIRIT: "For Christ…being put to death in the flesh but quickened by the Spirit" (1 Pet. 3:18).

"But if the Spirit of him that raised up Jesus from the dead dwell in you, he that raised up Christ from the dead shall also quicken your mortal bodies by his Spirit that dwelleth in you" (Rom. 8:11).

THEY HEAL:

FATHER: "Heal me, O LORD, and I shall be healed; save me, and I shall be saved" (Jer. 17:14).

"For I will restore health unto thee, and I will heal thee of thy wounds, saith the Lord" (Jer. 30:17).

<u>JESUS</u>: "And Jesus went about all Galilee…healing all manner of sickness and all manner of disease among the people" (Matt. 4:23).

"And he cast out the spirits with *his* word, and healed all that were sick" (Matt. 8:16).

<u>HOLY SPIRIT</u>: "For to one is given by the Spirit the word of wisdom…To another the gifts of healing by the same Spirit" (1 Cor. 12:8–9).

THEY SAVE:

<u>FATHER</u>: "Behold, God *is* my salvation" (Isa. 12:2).

"For the grace of God that bringeth salvation hath appeared to all men" (Titus 2:11).

<u>JESUS</u>: "Thou shalt call his name Jesus: for he shall save his people from their sins" (Matt. 1:21).

"Believe on the Lord Jesus Christ, and thou shalt be saved" (Acts 16:31).

<u>HOLY SPIRIT</u>: "He saved us, by the washing of regeneration, and renewing of the Holy Ghost" (Titus 3:5).

THEY ARE GRACE:

<u>FATHER</u>: "For the grace of God that bringeth salvation hath appeared to all men" (Titus 2:11).

"But the God of all grace, who hath called us into his eternal glory by Christ Jesus" (1 Pet. 5:10).

<u>JESUS</u>: "Grace and truth came by Jesus Christ" (John 1:17).

"The grace of God, and the gift by grace, *which is* by one man, Jesus Christ hath abounded unto many" (Rom. 5:15).

<u>HOLY SPIRIT</u>: "And I will pour upon the house of David...the spirit of grace and of supplications" (Zech. 12:10).

"Of how much sorer punishment, suppose ye, shall he be thought worthy, who hath trodden under foot the Son of God... and hath done despite unto the Spirit of grace?" (Heb. 10:29).

THEY ARE TRUTH:

<u>FATHER</u>: "A God of truth" (Deut. 32:4).

"God, that cannot lie" (Titus 1:2).

JESUS: "I am the way, the truth, and the life" (John 14:6).

"Grace and truth came by Jesus Christ" (John 1:17).

HOLY SPIRIT: "Howbeit when he, the Spirit of truth, is come, he will guide you into all truth" (John 16:13).

"And it is the Spirit that beareth witness, because the Spirit is truth" (1 John 5:6).

THEY SANCTIFY:

FATHER: "And God blessed the seventh day, and sanctified it" (Gen. 2:3).

"Say ye of him [Jesus], whom the Father hath sanctified" (John 10:36).

JESUS: "And ye shall keep my statutes, and do them: I *am* the LORD which sanctify you" (Lev. 20:8).

"For I the Lord do sanctify them" (Lev. 21:23).

HOLY SPIRIT: "That I [Paul] should be the minister of Jesus Christ…being sanctified by the Holy Ghost" (Rom. 15:16).

"Elect according to the foreknowledge of God the Father, through sanctification of the Spirit" (1 Pet. 1:2).

"Because God hath from the beginning chosen you to salvation through sanctification of the Spirit and belief of the truth" (2 Thess. 2:13).

THEY ARE COMFORTORS:

FATHER: "Blessed *be* God, even the Father of our Lord Jesus Christ, the Father of mercies, and the God of all comfort; Who comforteth us in all our tribulation" (2 Cor. 1:3–4).

"Now our Lord Jesus Christ himself, and God, even our Father, which hath loved us, and hath given *us* everlasting consolation and good hope through grace, comfort your hearts and stablish you in every good word and work" (2 Thess. 2:16–17).

JESUS: "He [Jesus] said, Daughter, be of good comfort; thy faith hath made thee whole" (Matt. 9:22).

"Now our Lord Jesus Christ himself… comfort your hearts and stablish you in every good word and work" (2 Thess. 2:16–17).

HOLY SPIRIT: "I [Jesus] will pray the Father, and he shall give you another Comforter, that he may abide with you for ever; *Even* the Spirit of truth" (John 14:16–17).

"But the Comforter, *which is* the Holy Ghost…" (John 14:26).

"Then had the churches rest…walking in the fear of the Lord, and in the comfort of the Holy Ghost" (Acts 9:31).

THEY GIVE PEACE:

FATHER: "And the peace of God, which passeth all understanding, shall keep your hearts and minds through Christ Jesus… and the God of peace shall be with you" (Phil. 4:7, 9).

"Grace *be* to you and peace from God our Father, and *from* the Lord Jesus Christ" (2 Cor 1:2).

JESUS: "Peace I leave with you, my peace I give unto you" (John 14:27).

HOLY SPIRIT: "But the Fruit of the Spirit is love, joy, peace" (Gal. 5:22).

THEY ARE FIRE:

<u>FATHER</u>: "And the sight of the glory of the Lord was like a devouring fire" (Exod. 24:17).

"For the LORD thy God *is* a consuming fire" (Deut. 4:24).

"The Ancient of days did sit…his throne *was like* a fiery flame, *and* his wheels *as* burning fire. A fiery stream issued and came forth from before him" (Dan. 7:9–10).

"The hand of the Lord GOD fell upon me. Then I beheld, and lo a likeness as the appearance of fire: from the appearance of his loins even downward, fire; and from his loins even upward, as the appearance of brightness" (Ezek. 8:1–2).

"For our God *is* a consuming fire" (Heb. 12:29).

<u>JESUS</u>: "When the Lord Jesus shall be revealed from heaven…in flaming fire" (2 Thess. 1:7–9).

"Then shall that Wicked be revealed, whom the Lord shall consume…and shall destroy with the brightness of his coming" (2 Thess. 2:8).

"But the day of the Lord will come…and the elements will melt with fervent, heat and the earth also and the works that are therein shall be burned up" (2 Pet. 3:10).

<u>HOLY SPIRIT</u>: "There appeared unto them cloven tongues like as of fire…and they were all filled with the Holy Ghost" (Acts 2:3–4).

"He shall baptize you with the Holy Ghost, and *with* fire" (Matt. 3:11).

MEMBERS OF THE GODHEAD HAVE PERSON CHARACTERISTICS

THEY HAVE MINDS:

<u>FATHER</u>: "Many, O LORD my God *are* thy wonderful works *which* thou hast done, and thy thoughts *which are* to us-ward" (Ps. 40:5).

"How precious also are thy thoughts unto me, O God!" (Ps. 139:17).

"For who hath known the mind of the Lord? or who hath been his counselor?" (Rom. 11:34).

<u>JESUS</u>: "For who hath known the mind of the Lord…but we have the mind of Christ" (1 Cor. 2:16).

"Let this mind be in you, which was also in Christ Jesus" (Phil. 2:5).

<u>HOLY SPIRIT</u>: "He that searcheth the hearts knoweth what *is* the mind of the Spirit" (Rom. 8:27).

THEY LOVE:

FATHER: "For God so loved the world, that he gave his only begotten Son" (John 3:16).

"For the Father himself loveth you" (John 16:27).

"God is love" (1 John 4:8).

JESUS: "Hereby perceive we the love *of God*, because he laid down his life for us" (1 John 3:16).

"This is my commandment, that ye love one another, as I have loved you" (John 15:12).

HOLY SPIRIT: "The fruit of the Spirit is love" (Gal. 5:22).

"Now I beseech you, brethren, for the Lord Jesus Christ's sake, and for the love of the Spirit, that ye strive together with me" (Rom. 15:30).

THEY SPEAK:

FATHER: "There came a voice from heaven, *saying*, thou art my beloved Son, in whom I am well pleased" (Mark 1:11).

"A voice out of the cloud, which said, This is my beloved Son, in whom I am well pleased; hear ye him" (Matt. 17:5).

JESUS: "Then spake Jesus again" (John 8:12).

"Jesus answered" (John 8:14, 19).

"Then said Jesus unto them" (John 8:28).

HOLY SPIRIT: "The Holy Ghost said, Separate me Barnabas and Saul" (Acts 13:2).

"It is not ye that speak, but the Holy Ghost" (Mark 13:11).

"When the Comforter is come…*even* the Spirit of truth, which proceedeth from the Father, he shall testify of me [Jesus]" (John 15:26).

"Howbeit when he, the Spirit of truth, is come…he shall not speak of himself; but whatsoever he shall hear, *that* shall he speak" (John 16:13).

THEY HAVE WILLS:

FATHER: "Our Father which art in heaven…Thy will be done in earth, as it is in heaven" (Matt. 6:9–10).

"For I came down from heaven, not to do mine own will, but the will of him that sent me. And this is the Father's will which hath sent me" (John 6:38–39).

"Father, if thou be willing, remove this cup from me: nevertheless not my will, but thine, be done" (Luke 22:42).

JESUS: "And Jesus put forth *his* hand, and touched him, saying, I will; be thou clean" (Matt. 8:3).

"O my Father…nevertheless not as I will, but as thou *wilt*" (Matt. 26:39).

Holy Spirit: "But all these worketh that one and the selfsame Spirit, dividing to every man severally as he will" (1 Cor. 12:11).

THEY HAVE EMOTIONS:

FATHER: "For God so loved the world, that He gave his only begotten Son" (John 3:16).

"These six *things* doth the LORD hate" (Prov. 6:16).

JESUS: "Jesus wept" (John 11:35).

"As the Father hath loved me, so have I [Jesus] loved you: continue ye in my love" (John 15:9).

HOLY SPIRIT: "But they rebelled, and vexed his holy Spirit" (Isa. 63:10).

"And grieve not the holy Spirit of God" (Eph. 4:30).

"Now I beseech you, brethren, for the Lord Jesus Christ's sake, and for the love of the Spirit, that ye strive together with me in *your* prayers to God for me" (Rom. 15:30).

"And ye became followers of us, and of the Lord, having received the word in much affliction, with joy of the Holy Ghost" (1 Thess. 1:6).

THEY TEACH:

FATHER: "And they shall be all taught of God. Every man therefore that hath heard, and hath learned of the Father, cometh unto me" (John 6:45).

"But as my Father hath taught me, I speak these things" (John 8:28).

<u>JESUS</u>: "And they were astonished at his [Jesus] doctrine: for he taught them as one that had authority, and not as the scribes" (Mark 1:22).

"And he [Jesus] began again to teach by the sea side…And he taught them many things" (Mark 4:1–2).

<u>HOLY SPIRIT</u>: "…which the Holy Ghost teacheth; comparing spiritual things with spiritual" (1 Cor. 2:13).

"But the Comforter, *which is* the Holy Ghost…he shall teach you all things" (John 14:26).

"For the Holy Ghost shall teach you in the same hour what ye ought to say" (Luke 12:12).

THEY LEAD AND GUIDE:

<u>FATHER</u>: "Our Father which art in heaven…lead us not into temptation" (Matt. 6:9, 13).

"For this God *is* our God for ever and ever: he will be our guide *even* unto death" (Ps. 48:14).

"…thou hast forsaken the LORD thy God, when he led thee by the way?" (Jer. 2:17).

JESUS: "Now God himself and our Father, and our Lord Jesus Christ, direct our way unto you" (1 Thess. 3:11).

"Behold, the Lord GOD will come…behold, his reward *is* with him…*and* gently lead those that are with young" (Isa. 40:10–11).

"And the LORD went before them by day in a pillar of a cloud, to lead them the way" (Exod. 13:21).

HOLY SPIRIT: "And Jesus being full of the Holy Ghost…was led by the Spirit into the wilderness" (Luke 4:1).

"Howbeit when he, the Spirit of truth, is come, he will guide you into all truth" (John 16:13).

"For as many as are led by the Spirit of God, they are sons of God…The Spirit itself beareth witness with our spirit, that we are children of God" (Rom. 8:14, 16).

"But if ye be led of the Spirit, ye and not under the law" (Gal. 5:18).

THEY GIVE GIFTS:

<u>FATHER</u>: "God hath dealt to every man the measure of faith" (Rom. 12:3).

"Every good gift and every perfect gift is from above, and commeth down from the Father of lights" (James 1:17).

"If ye then, being evil, know how to give good gifts unto your children: how much more shall your heavenly Father give the Holy Spirit to them that ask him?" (Luke 11:13).

<u>JESUS</u>: "When the Comforter is come, whom I [Jesus] will send unto you from the Father, *even* the Spirit of truth" (John 15:26).

"Unto every one of us is given grace according to the measure of the gift of Christ. Wherefore he saith, when he ascended up on high...and gave gifts unto men" (Eph. 4:7–8).

"And he [Jesus] gave some, apostles; and some, prophets; and some, evangelists; and some, pastors and teachers" (Eph. 4:11).

<u>HOLY SPIRIT</u>: "For to one is given by the Spirit the word of wisdom; to another the word of knowledge by the same Spirit… to another the working of miracles; to another prophecy" (1 Cor. 12:8–11).

THE GODHEAD IS LOVE

The Godhead is love. He is omnipotent, omniscient, omnipresent, eternal, holy, power, and creator. He gives life and resurrects. He is truth, glory, grace, and dwells in us. He sanctifies, comforts, and has a mind. He wills, feels, teaches, leads, guides, gives gifts, intercedes, saves, and is seen as light and fire.

The Godhead is love, and since love must have a recipient, God the Father, God the Son, and God the Holy Spirit have infinite love between themselves with no self-seeking, each glorifying the other. They sought to share themselves and this unselfish love with other intelligent creatures, so they created beings, angels, and mankind to benefit from and reciprocate love to the Godhead and each other. If one becomes the recipient of his own love, then he is self-centered, selfish, egotistical, and proud. This leads to sin (sinful thoughts and sinful actions), separation from God and death. "But your iniquities have separated between you and your God, and your sins have hid his face from you, that he will not hear" (Isa. 59:2).

The Godhead is one in purpose, mind, and character. The Omnipotent Godhead used their power and omniscience to design natural laws and the matter that obeys these laws and upholds all their creation with their omnipresence. These natural laws are not only scientific laws but moral laws. The Bible is filled with God's moral law and examples of keeping it and breaking it.

The Godhead can be summarized by one Greek word, *agape* (God like love).

"He that loveth not knoweth not God; for God is love...God is love; and he that dwelleth in love dwelleth in God, and God in him...We love him because he first loved us" (1 John 4:8, 16, 19).

"If a man love me, he will keep my words: and my Father will love him, and we will come unto him, and make our abode with him" (John 14:23).

"Charity…seeketh not her own" (1 Cor. 13:4–5).

"Let no one seek his own, but each one the other's *well-being*" (1 Cor. 10:24, NKJV).

"In lowliness of mind let each esteem other better than themselves" (Phil. 2:3).

"*Be* kindly affectioned one to another with brotherly love; in honor preferring one another" (Rom. 12:10).

"Submitting yourselves one to another in the fear of God" (Eph. 5:21).

"Put on therefore, as the elect of God, holy and beloved, bowels of mercies, kindness, humbleness of mind, meekness, longsuffering; Forbearing one another, and forgiving one another…even as Christ forgave you, so also *do* ye. And above all these things *put on* charity, which is the bond of perfectness…And whatsoever ye do in word or deed, *do* all in the name of the Lord Jesus, giving thanks to God and the Father by him" (Col. 3:12–14, 17).

"For I [Jesus] do always those things that please him [the Father]" (John 8:29).

"We...ought to bear the infirmities of the weak, and not to please ourselves...For even Christ pleased not himself" (Rom. 15:1, 3).

"Therefore we make it our aim...to be well pleasing to Him [Christ]" (2 Cor. 5:9, NKJV).

"He has shown you, O man, what *is* good; and what does the LORD require of you but to do justly, to love mercy, and to walk humbly with your God" (Mic. 6:8, NKJV).

"Pure religion and undefiled before God and the Father is this, To visit the fatherless and widows in their affliction, *and* to keep himself unspotted from the world" (James 1:27).

"Learn to do good; seek justice, rebuke the oppressor; defend the fatherless, plead for the widow" (Isa. 1:17, NKJV).

"The LORD watches over the strangers; He relieves the fatherless and widow" (Ps. 146:9, NKJV).

"And be ye kind one to another, tenderhearted, forgiving one another, even as

God for Christ's sake hath forgiven you" (Eph. 4:32).

"By love serve one another" (Gal. 5:13).

"As we have therefore opportunity, let us do good unto all *men*" (Gal. 6:10).

"Let us consider one another to provoke unto love and good works" (Heb. 10:24).

JESUS GAVE HIS LIFE AS AN EXAMPLE OF THE LOVE OF THE GODHEAD

"Be ye therefore followers of God, as dear children; and walk in love, as Christ also hath loved us, and hath given himself for us an offering and a sacrifice to God for a sweetsmelling savor" (Eph. 5:1–2).

"Even as the Son of man came not to be ministered unto, but to minister, and to give his life a ransom for many" (Matt. 20:28).

"Christ died for the ungodly...But God commendeth his love toward us, in that, while we were yet sinners, Christ died for us" (Rom. 5:6, 8).

"I am the good shepherd: the good shepherd giveth his life for the sheep...As the Father knoweth me, even so know I the Father: and I lay down my life for the sheep...Therefore doth my Father love me, because I lay down my life" (John 10:11, 15, 17).

"God will provide himself a lamb for a burnt offering" (Gen. 22:8).

"So Christ was once offered to bear the sins of many" (Heb. 9:28).

GOD'S MORAL LAW CAN ALSO BE SUMMARIZED BY ONE GREEK WORD—AGAPE (GODLIKE LOVE)

"For all the law is fulfilled in one word, *even* in this; Thou shalt love thy neighbor as thyself" (Gal. 5:14).

"Love worketh no ill to his neighbor: therefore love *is* the fulfilling of the law" (Rom. 13:10).

"If ye fulfill the royal law according to the scripture, Thou shalt love thy neighbor as thyself, ye do well" (James 2:8).

"Therefore all things whatsoever ye would that men should do to you, do ye even so to them: for this is the law and the prophets" (Matt. 7:12).

"Bear ye one another's burdens, and so fulfil the law of Christ" (Gal. 6:2).

"A new commandment I [Jesus] give unto you, that ye love one another; as I have loved you, that ye also love one another" (John 13:34).

"If a man say, I love God, and hateth his brother, he is a liar...and this commandment have we from him, that he who loveth God love his brother also" (1 John 4:20–21).

"Greater love hath no man than this, that a man lay down his life for his friends" (John 15:13).

"But I say unto you, Love your enemies, bless them that curse you, do good to them that hate you, and pray for them which despitefully use you, and persecute you" (Matt. 5:44).

"For if, when we were enemies, we were reconciled to God by the death of his Son, much more, being reconciled, we shall be saved by his life" (Rom. 5:10).

"And *one* shall say unto him [Jesus], What *are* these wounds in thine hands? Then he shall answer, *Those* with which I was wounded *in* the house of my friends" (Zech. 13:6).

JESUS SUMMARIZED THIS ONE WORD MORAL LAW—AGAPE (GODLIKE LOVE)—AS TWO COMMANDMENTS:

"Jesus said unto him, Thou shalt love the Lord thy God with all thy heart, and with all thy soul, and with all thy mind. This is the first and great commandment. And the second *is* like unto it, Thou shalt love thy neighbor as thyself. On these two commandments hang all the law and the prophets" (Matt. 22:37–40). Jesus was quoting the Old Testament scriptures.

"Thou shalt love the LORD thy God with all thine heart, and with all thy soul, and with all thy might" (Deut. 6:5).

"Thou shalt love thy neighbor as thyself: I *am* the Lord" (Lev. 19:18).

THE GOD ENLARGED THE TWO LAWS TO THE TEN COMMANDMENTS:

God enlarged these two laws to make it easier for us to understand and do them by speaking them from Mount Sinai. These are known as the Ten Commandments found in Exodus 20:3–17 and Deuteronomy 5:7–21. A short time later, God called

Moses into the mount and gave him the tablets of stone upon which he had written his law (Exod. 24:12). These two tables of stone were written with the finger of God (Exod. 31:18). God also stipulated "Ye shall not add unto the word which command you, neither shall ye diminish *ought* from it, that ye may keep the commandments of the LORD your God which I command you" (Deut. 4:2). As we look at these Ten Commandments we see the recipient of the first four commandments is the Godhead.

"Thou shalt love the LORD thy God with all thine heart, and with all thy soul, and with all thy might" (Deut. 6:5).

We see the recipient of the last 6 commandments our neighbors, whether friends or enemies. "Thou shalt love thy neighbor as thyself: I *am* the Lord" (Lev. 19:18). Scripture shows:

THE GODHEAD IS LOVE, THE GODHEAD'S CHARACTER IS LOVE, AND THE GODHEAD'S LAW IS LOVE.

THE GODHEAD DOES NOT CHANGE

"For I *am* the LORD, I change not" (Mal. 3:6).

"Jesus Christ the same yesterday, and to day, and for ever" (Heb. 13:8).

"I know that, whatsoever God doeth, it shall be for ever: nothing can be put to it, nor any thing taken from it" (Eccles. 3:14).

"My God…thy years *are* throughout all generations. Of old hast thou laid the foundation of the earth: and the heavens *are* the work of thy hands. They shall perish, but thou shalt endure…thou *art* the same, and thy years shall have no end" (Ps. 102:24–27).

"The counsel of the LORD standeth for ever, the thoughts of his heart to all generations" (Ps. 33:11).

"Every good gift and every perfect gift is from above, and cometh down from the

Father of lights, with whom is no variableness, neither shadow of turning" (James 1:17).

THE GODHEAD'S WORD DOES NOT CHANGE:

"The grass withereth, the flower fadeth: but the word of our God shall stand for ever" (Isa. 40:8).

"But the word of the Lord endureth for ever" (1 Pet. 1:25).

"Heaven and earth shall pass away: but my [Jesus'] words shall not pass away" (Luke 21:33).

"My [God's] covenant will I not break, nor alter the thing that is gone out of my lips" (Ps. 89:34).

"The works of his hands *are* verity and judgment; all his commandments *are* sure. They stand fast for ever and ever, *and are* done in truth and uprightness" (Ps. 111:7–8).

"For verily I [Jesus] say unto you, Till heaven and earth pass, one jot or one tittle shall in no wise pass from the law" (Matt. 5:18).

BIBLICAL DEFINITION OF SIN

"Whosoever committeth sin transgresseth also the law: for sin is the transgression of the law" (1 John 3:4).

"All unrighteousness is sin" (1 John 5:17).

"Therefore to him that knoweth to do good, and doeth *it* not, to him it is sin" (James 4:17).

"If ye have respect to persons, ye commit sin, and are convinced of the law as transgressors" (James 2:9).

"He that despiseth his neighbor sinneth: but he that hath mercy on the poor, happy *is* he" (Proverbs 14:21).

"A high look, and a proud heart...*is* sin" (Prov. 21:4).

"The thought of foolishness *is* sin" (Prov. 24:9).

"Whatsoever *is* not of faith is sin" (Rom. 14:23).

"Flee fornication. Every sin that a man doeth is without the body; but he that committeth fornication sinneth against his own body" (1 Cor. 6:18).

"Rebellion *is as* the sin of witchcraft, and stubbornness *is as* iniquity and idolatry" (1 Sam. 15:23).

WHERE SIN ORIGINATED

Scripture indicates sin originated in heaven with a created angel called a covering cherub.

"Thou art the anointed cherub that covereth…Thou wast perfect in thy ways from the day thou wast created, till iniquity was found in thee…Thine heart was lifted up because of thy beauty, thou hast corrupted thy wisdom by reason of thy brightness" (Ezek. 28:14–15, 17).

"And there was war in heaven: Michael and his angels fought against the dragon; and the dragon fought and his angels, and prevailed not; neither was their place found any more in heaven. And the great dragon was cast out, that old serpent called the Devil, and Satan, which deceiveth the whole world: he was cast out into the earth, and his angels were cast out with him" (Rev. 12:7–9).

"How art thou fallen from heaven, O Lucifer...for thou hast said in thine heart. I will ascend into heaven, I will exalt my throne above the stars of God... I will become like the most High" (Isa. 14:12–14). Pride, rebellion, putting self before God and other sins caused Lucifer, the dragon, serpent, Devil, and Satan, to be cast to the earth with one-third of heaven's angels who believed, trusted, and sided with Lucifer in his self-love and rebellion against their Creator. What have Lucifer and his fallen angels been doing since they have been on earth? They do the same thing they did in heaven, turning created beings to love of self and away from the Godhead, their Creator. Eve was deceived and stole fruit from the tree of knowledge of good and evil, trusting the lies of the serpent, Satan.

"Ye shall not surely die" (Gen. 3:4). Instead of trusting God's <u>unchanging</u> Word, "For in the day that thou eatest thereof thou shalt surely die" (Gen. 2:17).

"For the wages of sin *is* death" (Rom. 6:23). Adam's love for Eve was greater than his love for God, so he also ate the fruit from the forbidden tree.

"Wherefore, as by one man sin entered into the world, and death by sin; and so death passed upon all men" (Rom. 5:12). This death was not just from illness, accident, and old age, but also murder. Cain demonstrated this when he killed his own brother, Abel. Jesus spoke the truth when he called the devil a murderer.

"He was a murderer from the beginning, and...a liar and the father of it" (John 8:44). Our Godhead of love inspired Paul to warn us also.

"For we wrestle not against flesh and blood, but against principalities, against powers, against rulers of darkness of this world, against spiritual wickedness in high *places*" (Eph. 6:12).

LOVE TURNED INWARD RESULTS IN SIN

The law of love is selfless love—other-centered love—a law of giving. We cannot be the recipient of our own love, for that results in sin.

"This know also, that in the last days perilous times shall come. For men shall be lovers of their own selves…without natural affection…lovers of pleasure more that lovers of God" (2 Tim. 3:1–2, 4).

"Let no man say when he is tempted, I am tempted of God: for God cannot be tempted with evil, neither tempteth he any man: But every man is tempted, when he is drawn away of his own lust, and enticed. Then when lust hath conceived, it bringeth forth sin: and sin when it is finished, bringeth forth death" (James 1:13–15).

"Keep thy heart with all diligence; for out of it *are* the issues of life" (Prov. 4:23).

"For as he thinketh in his heart, so *is* he" (Prov. 23:7).

"And GOD saw that the wickedness of man *was* great in the earth, and *that* every imagination of the thoughts of his heart *was* only evil continually" (Gen. 6:5).

"The heart *is* deceitful above all *things*, and desperately wicked: who can know it" (Jer. 17:9).

"A good man out of the good treasure of his heart bringeth forth that which is good; and an evil man out of the evil treasure of his heart bringeth forth that which is evil: for out of the abundance of the heart his mouth speaketh" (Luke 6:45).

"That which cometh out of the man, that defileth the man. For from within, out of the heart of men, proceed evil thoughts, adulteries, fornications, murders, thefts, covetousness, wickedness, deceit, lasciviousness, an evil eye, blasphemy, pride, foolishness: All these evil things come from within, and defile the man" (Mark 7:20–23).

"Thine [Lucifer's] heart was lifted up because of thy beauty, thou hast corrupted thy wisdom by reason of thy brightness" (Ezek. 28:17).

"This people draweth nigh to me with their mouth, and honoreth me with *their* lips; but their heart is far from me, but in vain they do worship me, teaching *for* doctrine the commandments of men" (Matt. 15:8–9).

"For with their mouth they show much love, *but* their heart goeth after covetousness" (Ezek. 33:31).

"There is a way which seemeth right unto a man, but the end thereof *are* the ways of death" (Prov. 14:12).

"Unto the pure all things *are* pure: but unto them that are defiled and unbelieving *is* nothing pure; but even their mind and conscience is defiled. They profess that they know God; but in works they deny *him*, being abominable, and disobedient, and unto every good work reprobate" (Titus 1:15–16).

SOME OF THE GODHEAD'S WORDS THAT HELP US OVERCOME THE SIN OF LOVE TURNED INWARD

"And thou shalt love the LORD thy God with all thine heart, and with all thy soul, and with all thy might" (Deut. 6:5).

"Thou shalt love thy neighbor as thyself" (Lev. 19:18).

"But seek ye first the kingdom of God, and his righteousness" (Matt. 6:33).

"Seek the LORD and His strength, seek his face continually" (1 Chron. 16:11).

"*There is* therefore now no condemnation to them which are in Christ Jesus, who walk not after the flesh, but after the Spirit…to be spiritually minded is life and peace… ye are not in the flesh, but in the Spirit, if so be that the Spirit of God dwell in you…for as many as are led by the Spirit of God, they are the sons of God" (Rom. 8:1, 6, 9, 14).

"But put ye on the Lord Jesus Christ, and make not provision for the flesh to *fulfill* the lusts *thereof*" (Rom. 13:14).

"And they that are Christ's have crucified the flesh with the affections and lusts. If we live in the Spirit, let us also walk in the Spirit" (Gal. 5:24–25).

"The world passeth away, and the lust thereof; but he that doeth the will of God abideth for ever" (1 John 2:17).

"Wherefore come out from among them, and be ye separate, saith the Lord, and touch not the unclean *thing*; and I will receive you" (2 Cor. 6:17).

"Submit yourselves therefore to God. Resist the devil, and he will flee from you. Draw nigh to God, and he will draw nigh to you. Cleanse *your* hands, *ye* sinners; and purify *your* hearts" (James 4:7–8).

"And be not conformed to this world: but be ye transformed by the renewing of your mind, that ye may prove what *is* that good and acceptable, and perfect, will of God" (Rom. 12:2).

"Let this mind be in you, which was also in Christ Jesus" (Phil. 2:5).

"Thou wilt keep *him* in perfect peace, *whose* mind *is* stayed *on thee*" (Isa. 26:3).

"Abstain from all appearance of evil" (1 Thess. 5:22).

"I will set no wicked thing before mine eyes" (Ps. 101:3).

"Let the words of my mouth, and the meditation of my heart, be acceptable in thy sight, O LORD, my strength, and my redeemer" (Ps. 19:14).

"Finally, brethren, whatsoever things are true, whatsoever things *are* honest, whatsoever things *are* just, whatsoever things *are* pure, whatsoever things *are* lovely, whatsoever things *are* of good report; if *there be* any virtue, and if *there* be any praise, think on these things" (Phil. 4:8).

THE GODHEAD PLEADS FOR OUR REPENTANCE

"The Lord…is longsuffering to us-ward, not willing that any should perish, but that all should come to repentance" (2 Pet. 3:9).

"Turn unto me, saith the LORD of hosts, and I will turn unto you, saith the Lord of hosts" (Zech. 1:3).

"The LORD your God *is* gracious and merciful, and will not turn away *his* face from you, if you return unto him" (2 Chron. 30:9).

"Let the wicked forsake his ways, and the unrighteous man his thoughts: and let him return unto the LORD and he will have mercy upon him; and to our God, for he will abundantly pardon" (Isa. 55:7).

"The *righteous* cry, and the LORD heareth, and delivereth them out of all their troubles. The LORD *is* nigh unto them that are of a broken heart; and saveth such as be of a contrite heart" (Ps. 34:17–18).

"Return, ye backsliding children, *and* I will heal your backslidings. Behold, we come unto thee; for thou *art* the LORD our God" (Jer. 3:22).

"But if the wicked will turn from all his sins that he hath committed, and keep all my statutes, and do which is lawful and right, he shall surely live, he shall not die" (Ezek. 18:21).

"Have I any pleasure at all that the wicked should die? saith the Lord GOD: *and* not that he should return from his ways, and live" (Ezek. 18:23).

"Repent, and turn *yourselves* from all your transgressions; so iniquity shall not be your ruin. Cast away from you all your transgressions, whereby ye have transgressed, and make you a new heart and a new spirit: for why will ye die…for I have no pleasure in the death of him that dieth, saith the Lord God: wherefore turn yourselves, and live" (Ezek. 18:30–32).

"Therefore also now, saith the LORD, turn ye *even* to me with all your heart, and with fasting, and with weeping, and with mourning: and rend your heart, and not your garments, and turn unto the LORD your God: for he *is* gracious and merciful, slow to anger and of great kindness, and repenteth him of the evil" (Joel 2:12–13).

"Even from the days of your fathers ye are gone away from mine ordinances, and have not kept *them*. Return unto me, and I will return unto you saith the LORD of hosts" (Mal. 3:7).

"Return unto me; for I have redeemed thee…Thus saith the Lord thy redeemer" (Isa. 44:22, 24).

"O Israel, return unto the LORD thy God; for thou hast fallen by thine iniquity… I will heal their backsliding, I will love them freely" (Hosea 14:1–4).

"*As* I live, saith the Lord GOD, I have no pleasure in the death of the wicked; but that the wicked turn from his way and live: turn ye, turn ye from your evil ways; for why will ye die" (Ezek. 33:11).

"For this *is* good and acceptable in the sight of God our Savior; who will have all men to be saved, and to come unto the knowledge of the truth" (1 Tim. 2:3–4).

THE GODHEAD PROMISES GOOD AND WELL-BEING TO ALL WHO KEEP THEIR COMMANDMENTS

"Only be thou strong and very courageous, that thou mayest observe to do according to all the law, which Moses my servant commanded thee: turn not from it *to* the right hand or *to* the left, that thou mayest prosper whithersoever thou goest. This book of the law shall not depart out of thy mouth; but thou shalt meditate therein day and night, that thou mayest observe to do according to all that is written therein: for then thou shalt make thy way prosperous, and that thou shalt have good success" (Josh. 1:7–8).

"Know therefore this day, and consider *it* in thine heart, that the LORD he *is* God in heaven above, and upon the earth beneath: *there is* none else. Thou shalt keep therefore his statutes, and his commandments, which I command thee this day, that it may go well with thee, and thy children after thee" (Deut. 4:39–40).

"And now, Israel, what doth the LORD thy God require of thee, but to fear the LORD thy God, to walk in all his ways, and to love him, and to serve the LORD thy God with all thy heart and with all thy soul, to keep the commandments of the LORD, and his statutes, which I command thee this day for thy good?" (Deut. 10:12–13).

"And the LORD thy God will make thee plenteous in every work of thine hand, in the fruit of thy body, and the fruit of thy cattle, and in the fruit of thy land, for good: for the LORD will again rejoice over thee for good, as he rejoiced over thy fathers: If thou shalt hearken unto the voice of the LORD thy God to keep his commandments and his statutes which are written in this book of the law, *and* if thou turn unto the LORD thy God with all thine heart, and with all thy soul" (Deut. 30:9–10).

"Blessed *is* the man *that* feareth the LORD, *that* delighteth greatly in his commandments" (Ps. 112:1).

"If ye be willing and obedient, ye shall eat the good of the land" (Isa. 1:19).

"But this thing commanded I them, saying, Obey my voice, and I will be your God, and ye shall be my people: and walk ye in all the ways that I have commanded you, that it may be well unto you" (Jer. 7:23).

THE GODHEAD DESIRES ALL TO BE SAVED

"For this *is* good and acceptable in the sight of God our Saviour; who will have all men be saved…who gave himself a ransom for all" (1 Tim. 2:3–4, 6).

"And we have seen and do testify that the Father sent the Son *to be* the Savior of the world" (1 John 4:14).

"For God so loved the world, that he gave his only begotten Son, that whosoever believeth in him should not perish, but have everlasting life…but that the world through him might be saved" (John 3:16–17).

"For the Son of man is come to save that which was lost…Even so it is not the will of your Father which is in heaven, that one of these little ones should perish" (Matt. 18:11, 14).

"But God commendeth his love toward us, in that, while we were yet sinners, Christ died for us...we were reconciled to God by the death of his Son, much more, being reconciled, we shall be saved by his life" (Rom. 5:8–10).

"Believe on the Lord Jesus Christ, and thou shalt be saved" (Acts 16:31).

"For whosoever shall call upon the name of the Lord shall be saved" (Rom. 10:13).

"And ye shall be hated of all *men* for my name's [Jesus'] sake: but he that endureth to the end shall be saved" (Matt. 10:22).

"Whosoever will lose his life for my [Jesus] sake shall find it" (Matt. 16:25).

"The Lord...is long suffering to us-ward, not willing that any should perish, but that all should come to repentance" (2 Pet. 3:9).

THE GODHEAD'S WARNINGS TO ALL WHO SIN, AND KEEP NOT THEIR COMMANDMENTS

"If I regard iniquity in my heart, the Lord will not hear *me*" (Ps. 66:18).

"He that turneth away his ear from hearing the law, even his prayer *shall be* abomination...He that covereth his sins shall not prosper: but whoso confesseth and forsaketh *them* shall have mercy" (Prov. 28:9, 13).

"But your iniquities have separated between you and your God, and your sins have hid *his* face from you, that he will not hear" (Isa. 59:2).

"Your iniquities have turned away these *things*, and your sins have withholden good *things* from you" (Jer. 5:25).

"Then shall they cry unto the LORD, but he will not hear them: he will even hide his face from them at that time, as they have behaved themselves ill in their doings" (Mic. 3:4).

"Yea, they made their hearts *as* an adamant stone, lest they should hear the law, and the words which the LORD of hosts hath sent in his spirit by the former prophets...therefore it is come to pass, *that* as he cried, and they would not hear; so they cried, and I would not hear, saith the LORD of hosts" (Zech. 7:12–13).

"For the eyes of the Lord *are* over the righteous, and his ears *are* open unto their prayers; but the face of the Lord *is* against them that do evil" (1 Pet. 3:12).

THE GODHEAD'S STRANGE ACT ON UNREPENTANT SELF-LOVERS

"Know ye not that the unrighteous shall not inherit the kingdom of God? Be not deceived: neither fornicators nor idolaters, nor adulterers, nor effeminate, nor abusers of themselves with mankind, nor thieves, nor covetous, nor drunkards, nor revilers, nor extortioners, shall inherit the kingdom of God" (1 Cor. 6:9–11).

"Now the works of the flesh are manifest, which are *these*; Adultery, fornication, uncleanness, lasciviousness, idolatry, witchcraft, hatred, variance, emulations, wrath, strife, seditions, heresies, envyings, murders, drunkenness, revellings, and such like...that they which do such things shall not inherit the kingdom of God" (Gal. 5:19–21).

"But fornication, and all uncleanness, or covetousness, let it not be once named among you, as becometh saints; neither filthiness, nor foolish talking, nor jesting, which are not convenient: but rather giving of thanks. For this you know, that no whoremonger, nor unclean person, nor covetous man, who is an idolater, hath any inheritance in the kingdom of Christ and of God" (Eph. 5:3–5).

"Blessed *are* they that do his commandments, that they may have right to the tree of life, and may enter in through the gates of the city. For without *are* dogs, and sorcerers, and whoremongers, and murderers, and idolaters, and whosoever loveth and maketh a lie" (Rev. 22:14–15).

"But the fearful, and unbelieving, and the abominable, and murderers, and whoremongers, and sorcerers, and idolaters, and all liars, shall have their part in the lake which burneth with fire and brimstone: which is the second death" (Rev. 21:8).

BIBLICAL EXPLANATION OF THE SECOND DEATH

"Turning the cities of Sodom and Gomorrah into ashes...making *them* an ensample unto those that after should live ungodly" (2 Pet. 2:6).

"And fire came down from God out of heaven, and devoured them. And the devil that deceived them was cast into the lake of fire...And death and hell were cast into the lake of fire. This is the second death. And whosoever was not found written in the book of life was cast into the lake of fire" (Rev. 20:9–10, 14–15).

"Thou [Lucifer] hast defiled thy sanctuaries by the multitude of thine iniquities... therefore will I bring forth a fire from the midst of thee, it shall devour thee, and I will bring thee to ashes upon the earth" (Ezek. 28:18).

"For, behold, the day cometh, that shall burn as an oven; and all the proud, yea, and all that do wickedly, shall be stubble: and the day that cometh shall burn them up, saith the LORD of hosts...And ye shall tread down the wicked; for they shall be ashes under the soles of your feet" (Mal. 4:1, 3).

"For the LORD thy God *is* a consuming fire" (Deut. 4:24).

"Who among us shall dwell with the devouring fire? Who among us shall dwell with everlasting burnings? He that walketh righteously, and speaketh uprightly; he that despiseth the gain of oppressions, that shaketh his hands from holding of bribes that...shutteth his eyes from seeing evil... thine eyes shall see the king in his beauty" (Isa. 33:14–15, 17).

"Mortify therefore your members which are upon the earth; fornication, uncleanness, inordinate affection, evil concupiscence, and covetousness, which is idolatry...But now ye also put off all these; anger, wrath, malice, blasphemy, filthy communication out of your mouth" (Col. 3:5, 9).

"This know also, that in the last days perilous times shall come. For men shall be lovers of their own selves, covetous, boasters, proud, blasphemers, disobedient to parents, unthankful, unholy, without natural affection, trucebreakers, false accusers, incontinent, fierce, despisers of those that are good, traitors, heady, highminded, lovers of pleasures more than lovers of God; Having a form of godliness, but denying the power thereof: from such turn away" (2 Tim. 3:1–5).

"Wherefore lay apart all filthiness and superfluity of naughtiness, and receive with meekness the engrafted word, which is able to save your souls" (James 1:21–22).

"He that overcometh shall not be hurt of the second death" (Rev. 2:11).

"Blessed and holy *is* he that hath part in the first resurrection: on such the second death hath no power, but they shall be priests of God and of Christ, and shall reign with him a thousand years" (Rev. 20:6).

WRITERS INSPIRED BY THE GODHEAD GIVE EXAMPLES OF PEOPLE THAT DELIGHT THEM

"Thus saith the LORD, Let not the wise *man* glory in his wisdom, neither let the mighty *man* glory in his might, let not the rich *man* glory in his riches: But let him that glorieth glory in this, that he understandeth and knoweth me" (Jer. 9:23–24).

"Noah found grace in the eyes of the LORD...Noah was a just man...*and* walked with God" (Gen. 6:8–9).

"For I [the Lord] know him [Abraham], that he will command his children and his household after him, and they shall keep the way of the LORD, to do justice and judgment" (Gen. 18:19).

"*Art* not thou our God, *who* didst drive out the inhabitants of this land...and gavest it to the seed of Abraham thy friend" (2 Chron. 20:7).

"The LORD said unto Satan, Hast thou considered my servant Job, for *there is* none like him in the earth, a perfect and an upright man, one that feareth God, and escheweth evil?" (Job 1:8).

"Hear now my words: If there be a prophet among you, *I* the LORD will make myself known unto him in a vision, *and* will speak unto him in a dream. My servant Moses *is* not so, who *is* faithful in all mine house. With him will I speak mouth to mouth" (Num. 12:6–7).

"If it seem evil unto you to serve the LORD, choose you this day whom ye will serve…but as for me and my house, we will serve the LORD" (Josh. 24:15).

"The LORD called Samuel: and he answered, Here *am* I…Samuel answered, Speak; for thy servant heareth" (1 Sam. 3:4, 10).

"Before his translation he had this testimony, that he [Enoch] pleased God" (Heb. 11:5).

"Enoch walked with God; and he *was* not, for God took him" (Gen. 5:24).

"He [God] raised up unto them David to be their king; to whom also he gave testimony, and said, I have found David the *son* of Jesse, a man after mine own heart, which shall fulfill all my will" (Acts 13:22).

"And he [Hezekiah] did *that which was* right in the sight of the LORD…He trusted in the LORD God…he clave to the LORD, *and* departed not from following him, but kept his commandments, which the LORD commanded Moses. And the LORD was with him" (1 Kings 18:3, 5–7).

"Daniel purposed in his heart that he would not defile himself" (Dan. 1:8).

"And he [Gabriel] informed *me*, and talked with me…I am come to shew *thee*; for thou *art* greatly beloved" (Dan. 9:22–23).

"As for these four children [Daniel, Hananiah, Mishael, and Azariah], God gave them knowledge and skill in all learning and wisdom" (Dan. 1:17).

"Did not we cast three men bound into the midst of the fire?…Lo, I see four men loose, walking in the midst of the fire… and the form of the fourth is like the Son of God" (Dan. 3:24–25).

"And the child [Jesus] grew, and waxed strong in spirit, filled with wisdom: and the grace of God was upon him" (Luke 2:40).

"But without faith *it is* impossible to please *him* [God]" (Heb. 11:6).

"Jesus also being baptized…And the Holy Ghost descended in a bodily shape like a dove upon him, and a voice came from heaven, which said, Thou art my beloved Son; in thee I am well pleased" (Luke 3:21–22).

"Jesus saw Nathanael coming to him, and saith of him, Behold an Israelite indeed, in whom is no guile!" (John 1:47).

APPENDIX 1

SOME BIBLICAL NAMES AND TITLES OF GOD THE FATHER:

"Lord" — Jeremiah 17:14; Daniel 9:4, 8, 19

"Lord our God" — Daniel 9:9, 14

"Lord of Lords" — 1 Timothy 6:15; Revelation 19:16

"Lord God" — Exodus 34:6; Daniel 9:3; Ezekiel 29: 8, 13, 20

"Most High God" — Genesis 14:18, 19, 20, 22; Mark 5:7; Acts 16:17

"Lord God Almighty" — Genesis 17:1; Revelation 4:8; 11:17; 21:22

"Everlasting God" — Genesis 21:33; Isaiah 40:28

"Eternal God" — Deuteronomy 33:27; 1 Timothy 1:17

"Living God" — Joshua 3:10; Hebrews 12:22; Revelation 7:2

"Father" — Matthew 26:42; Luke 23:34

"Heavenly Father" — Matthew 6:14, 26; 15:13; Luke 11:13

"God the Father" — 1 Thessalonians 1:1; Ephesians 6:23; 2 Peter 1:17; Jude 1

"Our Father which art in heaven" — Matthew 6:1, 9; 7:21

"Father of lights" — James 1:17

"Lord God of Hosts" — Psalm 80:7; Jeremiah 5:14; Amos 9:5

SOME BIBLICAL NAMES AND TITLES OF GOD THE SON, JESUS:

"The Christ" — Matthew 16:16: Mark 8:29; Luke 9:20; John 6:60

"Immanuel" — Matthew 1:23

"Messiah" — John 1:41; 4:25; Daniel 9:25, 26

"Redeemer" — Isaiah 59:20

"Savior" — Acts 5:31; Luke 2:11

"Son of God" — Luke 1:35

"Word of God" — John 1:1, 14:
 Revelation 19:13

"Son of man" — Matthew 8:20; Acts 7:56

"Lord of lords and King of kings" —
 Revelation 17:14

"Lamb of God" — John 1:29, 36;
 Revelation 5:6, 12

"Wonderful" — Isaiah 9:6

"Counselor" — Isaiah 9:6

"The mighty God" — Isaiah 9:6

"Prince of Peace" — Isaiah 9:6

"The everlasting Father" — Isaiah 9:6

"I Am" — John 8:58

"the Angel of God" — Genesis 31:11–13

"the Angel of the Lord" — Exodus 3:24

"An Angel of the Lord" —
 Judges 13:21–22

SOME BIBLICAL NAMES AND TITLES OF THE HOLY SPIRIT:

"Holy spirit" — Psalm 51:11; Luke 11:13

"Holy Ghost" — Matthew 1:18; Acts 5:3; 1 John 5:7

"Spirit of Truth" — John 14:17; 15:26; 16:13; 1 John 5:6

"Spirit of God" — Genesis 1:2; Matthew 3:16; Romans 8:9; John 20:22; Ephesians 4:30

"Spirit of the Lord" — 2 Corinthians 3:17; Isaiah 11:2; Acts 5:9

"Spirit of Christ" — Romans 8:9; 1 Peter 1:11

"Spirit of life" — Romans 8:2; Revelation 11:11

"The Sprit" — John 3:5, 6, 8, 34; Romans 3: 5, 9, 11, 23; 1 John 5:6, 8.

"Spirit of grace" — Zechariah 12:10; Hebrews 10:19

"Spirit of glory" — 1 Peter 4:14

"Good spirit" — Nehemiah 9:20

"Comforter" — John 14:16, 26;
15:26; 16:7

PERSONAL PRONOUNS (He, Him, Himself, His, Whom) USED FOR EACH MEMBER OF THE GODHEAD:

God the Father — Psalm 50:6; Amos 6:8; Isaiah 45:18; 2 Chronicles 13:12; John 14:7, 16; Revelation 21:3

God the Son — 1 Peter 2:21–24; Hebrews 2:14; 7:27; 9:26, 14; Titus 2:14; 1 Timothy 2:6; 1 Thessalonians 4:16; Philippians 2:7–8; Ephesians 2:20; Romans 15:3

The Holy Spirit, Comforter — John 14:16, 17, 26; 15:26; 16: 7, 8, 13, 14

THE DEFINITE ARTICLE 'THE' IS USED TO INDICATE THE FOLLOWING NOUN REFERS TO A UNIQUE PERSON:

God the Father: The Lord God—Genesis 2:4, 5, 7, 8, 9, 13, 14, 21, 22, 23; God the Father—2 John 3; the Father—Matthew 11:27; the Father—Mark 13:32: God the Lord—Isaiah

42:5; the high God–Psalm 78:35; the Most High—Psalm 50:14; the Father loveth the Son–John 3:35

God the Son: the Lamb—Revelation 15:3; the Son of God—Revelation 2:18; Jesus the Son of God—Hebrews 4:14; the Son of God—Luke 22:70; the Father loveth the Son—John 5:20; the Son of man—Matthew 12:32; the Lord Jesus Christ—Romans 15:30; the Lord of glory—2 Corinthians 2:8

The Holy Ghost and the Holy Spirit: the Holy Ghost—2 Peter 1:21; the Holy Ghost—I Peter 1:12; the Holy Ghost—Romans 5:5; Matthew 1:18, 20; 2 Timothy 1:14; Titus 3:5; Luke 1:35; he, the Spirit of truth—John 16:13; the Holy Ghost—Acts 9:17, 31; the Holy Ghost—I Thessalonians 1:5, 6; The Comforter which is the Holy Ghost—John 14:26; the Spirit—John 3:34

APPENDIX 2

THREE PERSONS OF THE GODHEAD IN ELLEN WHITE'S WRITINGS, THE SPIRIT OF PROPHECY:

Special Testimonies Series A:

"The prince of the power of evil can only be held in check by the power of God in the third Person of the Godhead, the Holy Spirit" (White 2013, p. 37).

"The eternal heavenly dignitaries-God, and Christ and the Holy Spirit-arming them [the disciples] with more than mortal energy...would advance with them to the work and convince the world of sin" (White 1901).

Special Testimonies Series B:

> The Father is all the fullness of the Godhead bodily, and is invisible to mortal sight. The Son is all the fullness

of the Godhead manifested. The Word of God declares Him to be "the express image of His person." "God so loved the world, that He gave His only begotten Son, that whosoever believeth in Him should not perish, but have everlasting life." Here is shown the personality of the Father. The Comforter that Christ promised to send after He ascended to heaven, is the Spirit in all the fullness of the Godhead, making manifest the power of divine grace to all who receive and believe in Christ as a personal Saviour. There are three living persons of the heavenly trio; in the name of these three great powers-the Father, the Son, and the Holy Spirit–those who receive Christ by living faith are baptized, and these powers will cooperate with the obedient subjects of heaven in their efforts to live the new life in Christ. (White 2013, pp. 62–63)

"We are to cooperate with the three highest powers in heaven, the Father, the Son, and the Holy Ghost, and these powers will work through us, making us workers together with God" (2013, p. 51).

"We know not who are the chosen of God only as they reveal the Education they have received from the Father and the Son through the Holy Spirit" (White 2013, p. 45).

Desire of Ages:

"Sin could be resisted and overcome only through the mighty agency of the third Person of the Godhead, who would come with no modified energy, but in the fullness of divine power" (White 1898, p. 671).

"Christ is about to depart to His home in the heavenly courts, but He assured His disciples that He would send them the Comforter, who would abide with them forever. To the guidance of this Comforter all may implicity trust…no circumstances, no distance, can separate us from the heavenly Comforter. Wherever we are, wherever we may go, He is always there, one given in Christ's place, to act in His stead" (1892, pp. 21–22).

Testimonies to Ministers:

"Evil had been accumulating for centuries and could only be restrained and resisted by the mighty power of the Holy Spirit, the third person of the Godhead who would come with no modified energy but in the fullness of divine power" (White 1900, p. 392).

That I May Know Him:

"Had God the Father come to our world and dwelt among us, humbling Himself, veiling His glory, that humanity might look upon Him, the history that we have of the life of Christ would not have been changed…In every act of Jesus, in every lesson of His instruction, we are to see and hear and recognize God in sight, in hearing, in effect it is the voice and movements of the Father" (White 1964).

Reflecting Christ

> "The Holy Spirit, sent in the name of Christ, was to teach them all things, and bring all things to their remembrance. The Holy Spirit was to be the

representative of Christ, the Advocate who is constantly pleading for the fallen race...He has assured you that the Holy Spirit was given to abide with you forever, to be your pleader and your guide. He asks you to trust in Him, and commit yourself into His keeping. The Holy Spirit is constantly at work, teaching, reminding, testifying, coming to the soul as a divine comforter, and convincing of sin as an appointed judge and guide." (White 1985, p. 129)

"Jesus said He would give us the Comforter. What is the Comforter? It is the Holy Spirit of God. What is the Holy Spirit? It is the representative of Jesus Christ, it is our advocate that stands by our side and places our petitions before the Father all fragrant with His merits...May the Holy Spirit of God impress the heart" (1985, p. 285).

"The Holy Spirit enabled the disciples to exalt the Lord alone, and guided the pens of the sacred historians, that the record of the words and works of Christ might be given to the world. Today this Spirit is constantly at work, seeking to draw the attention of men to the great sacrifice made upon the cross of Calvary to unfold to the word the love of God to man…The Spirit re-creates, refines and sanctifies human beings, fitting them to become members of the royal family, children of the heavenly king" (1985, p. 133).

Counsels on Health

"The Godhead was stirred with pity for the race, and the Father, the Son, and the Holy Spirit gave themselves to the working out of the plan of redemption. In order fully to carry out this plan it was decided that Christ, the only begotten Son of God should give Himself an offering for sin" (White 1923, p. 222).

Steps to Christ

"The heart of God yearned over His earthly children with a love stronger than death. In giving up His Son, He poured out to us all heaven in one gift. The Saviour's life and death and intercession, the ministry of angels, the pleading of the Spirit, the Father working above and through all, the unceasing interest of heavenly beings, all are enlisted in behalf of man's redemption" (White 1892, p. 21).

ABOUT THE AUTHOR

Elwin Shull is a graduate of Andrews University. He taught in Seventh-day Adventist schools for nearly forty years and retired after spending twenty of those years at Indiana Academy. He currently works at his local Adventist Book Center and conducts a correspondence Bible school for the Indiana Conference of Seventh-day Adventists.

TEACH Services, Inc.
P U B L I S H I N G
www.TEACHServices.com • (800) 367-1844

We invite you to view the complete
selection of titles we publish at:
www.TEACHServices.com

We encourage you to write us
with your thoughts about this,
or any other book we publish at:
info@TEACHServices.com

TEACH Services' titles may be
purchased in bulk quantities for
educational, fund-raising, business,
or promotional use.
bulksales@TEACHServices.com

Finally, if you are interested in
seeing your own book in print,
please contact us at:
publishing@TEACHServices.com

We are happy to review
your manuscript at no charge.

www.ingramcontent.com/pod-product-compliance
Lightning Source LLC
Chambersburg PA
CBHW072031170426
43200CB00025B/2553